FLIGHT

illustrated poetry

Leonor Alvim Brazão

I dedicate this flight to:

Maria Adélia Brazão,
for her support to publish these poems

Graciela Ibañez Sepulveda,
for her encouragement to write these lines

Leonor Alvim,
for her eternal inspiration

Translation by P. Doug Frey

A special thank you to P. Doug Frey, Luisa Alvim,
Maria Leonor Brazão and Mariana Brazão

Time stopped without pain
and without longing.
Together we learned again to exist.
For me, mourning was painted black.
With you, I learned
that it can have other colors,
That Presence
can have other forms,
And the color that
you wish to give it.

Silence

In silence you speak to me,
In silence you tell me,
That love remains,
That love exists.
In silence I hear you,
In silence,
With us,
Always present!

for Leonor, my mother

Soaring

I write
poetry unshackled
and without pretense.
Only the voice of my heart
which soars high
and tries
to get near
to another dimension.

Dream

I have a dream,
A song,
Made of words and letters,
Commas and action.
I have a dream,
A song,
A melody composed
With my syllables.
A musician,
A composer,
Who discovers the sweetness,
The rhythm of my poetry.
I have a dream,
That I will awaken
Wrapped up in this song!

for Antonio Celso

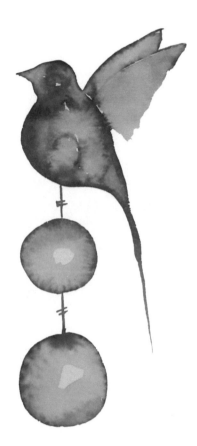

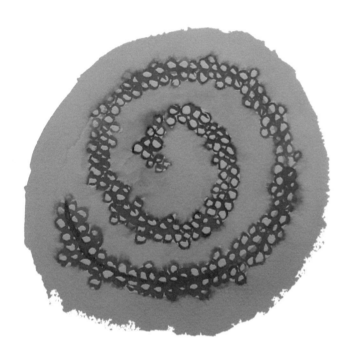

Poetry

I heal my soul
With pepper, parsley and nutmeg,
Ingredients and spices
That cure the pain that goes deep inside me.
Pure poetry,
That gives a taste
Of suffering.
Words that wander,
And fit themselves into rhymes,
Alternating,
By unfolding into prose,
Until they come to their end.
Where I bend in and ask:
What was the title of this story?

I Am Bird!

I am a bird of many colors,
Who likes to soar,
I take with me whoever can,
And knows how to glide.
From high, above, I take in the sky dimension,
Painted blue,
And earth painted yellow.
Other colors I see,
But those I keep,
For those who don't know how to soar!

The Past

I return to the land of my father
That today it is also mine.
I dry up the tears
Of the past,
I hear the color of its sound,
And make it present.

I look deeply into the sea,
In each wave a promise,
In each person a remembrance.

What was once my raging storm,
Has become sweet calmness,
The color of the sea remains the same,
But my view has changed.

for Ruy, my father

Time

Slowly, time unfolds.
A journey.
Large steps pave the trail
Not yet walked upon.
Slowly, time unfolds
If I look back.

Mirror

Through your eyes
I see mine,
that watch over you,
my mirror.

Memories that we carry
through an ocean of feelings.

In your eyes
I see myself,
a reflection of you.

Generations of emotions
that have depth in their eyes.

I look to you,
when you sense me.

In your eyes,
I see you as you
reflected in me.

Through my eyes
I see reflected,
the beauty that lives in you.

for Maria Leonor

Mine,

Ours.

Flight 12

The Journey

Follow your path,
Open your wings,
Soar above your dreams,
Learn to land,
In a safe harbor.
Don't be held back
By fierce storms,
And return one day,
To tell me your story,
The colors of your journey,
The love that you have gathered,
And the stones that you have learned to step on.

for Mariana

One Life

Up until the final breath
Everything has been worth it.
The breeze of the ocean,
The coming and going of the seven waves,
The promise of a new wave
Followed by dreams,
The desire for a better world.

On the pavement reality is raw.

But the breeze always blows
With hope.
The waves could have been eight
The magic wouldn't dissolve.
There, far away, towards the sun,
Lies a sea to explore.
With each turned page
A life renewed,
The music between the lines,
The dance on tiptoes,
The heaviness was only wind.
A leap,
A path,
A thicket within,
A discovery,
A tragedy,
One life!

Tropical Life

I like these people who want everything,
Can do everything.
I admire the sweat of their difficult life,
With hope for tomorrow.
I like the sensuality,
Their smile,
Which wakes up with the tone of the future.
I like these people,
Who sing the suffering,
Lifting the pain,
With the color of their art.
I like these people,
And their freedom.

Life Is Sweet

Ask me what is the color of a dream,
I respond with the sound of my reality.
The barriers that life imposes,
Are greater than my will.

A wall built,
Of tiles, cement, wind,
Disappointment,
Opposition.
A sea of difficulties.

One step forward,
Two sideways,
Diagonal waves, with dunes to explore.
I take off my shoes and I run again,
To swim free in the salty sea.

Because life is sweet,
If you protect your dream,
Without measuring the obstacles.

On the Ground

I am happy only
If I step on the ground.
I breathe the air,
I feel the wind,
And I feel the sun beating down,
On my tired body,
Filled with illusion.

One day the space
Will open up.
I will release this repressed flight,
Flying above the stars,
That I have contemplated.
An unreachable dream,
Which is only real
In my imagination.

I will believe,
I will wish,
and dream,
that this reality
Will always be my ground.

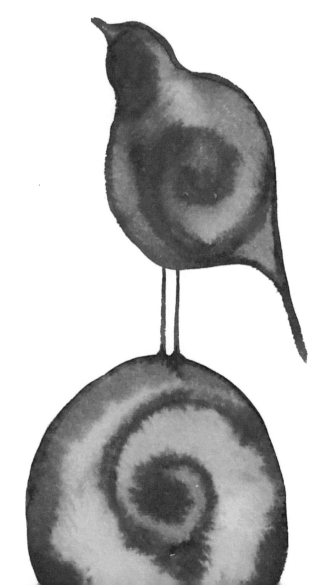

Flight 17

Longing

When time moves backwards,
Lifting the dust,
Playing the music,
Playing the longing,
Like Jazz from the past.
Worn melodies
Of joy and tears,
Made of moments
With sounds and smells,
Life and Death.

Everything departs, everything passes,
Everything lives, everything dies,
Everything is music,
When time moves backwards.

People Like Us

I paint, and I paint,
The smile of an unexpected meeting,
A hidden tear of a child,
Who lost his sweetness.
I paint, and I paint,
A mundane routine with a sunset,
Sweet,
With the taste of mint.
I paint, and I paint,
With taste, flavor and saliva,
Of people like us.
I paint, and I paint,
Day after day,
The longing of the passing day,
With hope for tomorrow.
I paint, and I paint,
Salt, sugar, sweat,
People who cry, people who laugh,
People who feel,
People just like us!

To Live

I know what it is to have,
I know what it is not to have,
I know what it is to give,
I know what it is to receive
Without return.

In the contemplation of life,
A pile of lines,
Unwritten,
With commas to be used.

In the contemplation of life,
Words used,
Words felt,
Paths crossed,
With a final ending.

I know what it is to have,
I know what it is to give,
I know,
Above all else, how to live!

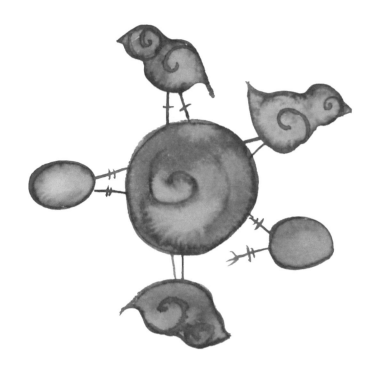

Faith

Paint your soul,
Sing your being,
Be inspired by little things.
Gather love with each look,
Live serenely,
Count the stars,
Step in the dew,
And let the sun dry you.
Believe,
That the colors of nature
Will give you eternal life,
And you will always,
be close to God.

for Maria Adélia

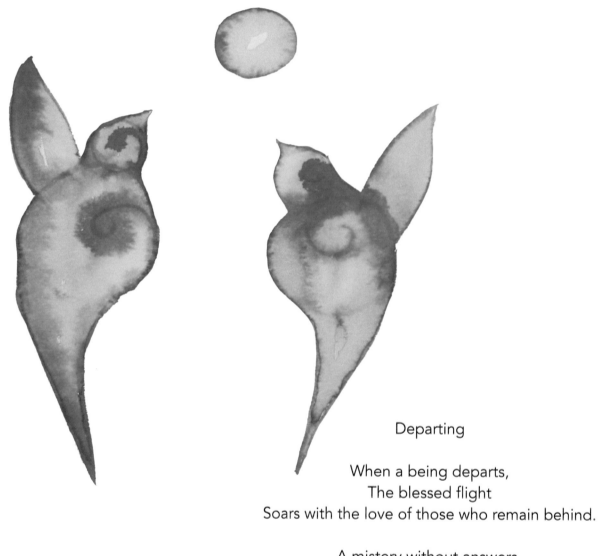

Departing

When a being departs,
The blessed flight
Soars with the love of those who remain behind.

A mistery without answers.
The light shines brightly on those who believe!

Flight 22

The poet

The soul of the poet,
Finds in words
his prayer.

Prayed verses,
mixed,
rhymed,
without limits.

On the horizon,
Is his wish,
His desire.

In his dream,
Is the ethereal poem,
Grasped only,
By the will of God!

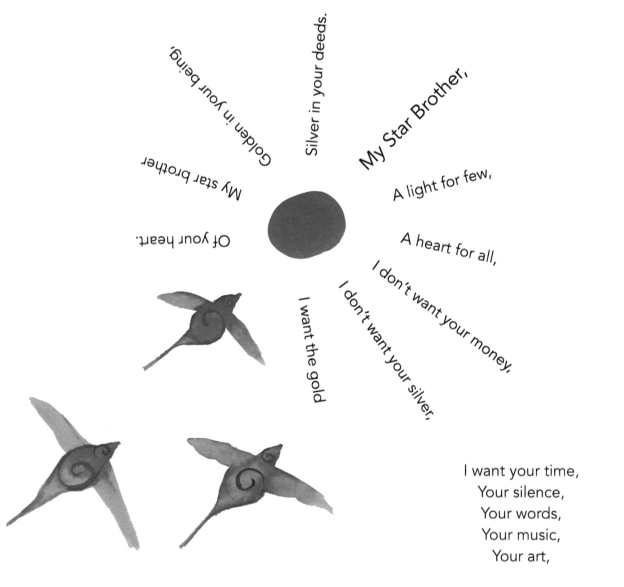

Silver in your deeds.

Golden in your being,

My star brother

Of your heart.

My Star Brother,

A light for few,

A heart for all,

I don't want your money,

I don't want your silver,

I want the gold

I want your time,
Your silence,
Your words,
Your music,
Your art,

I always want to be in your heart!

for Tomás, Rui and Luis

Flight 24

Rebellion

I like the freedom,
Of the wind that flows through my mind.
The breeze that lets me soar
In my thoughts.
Between images and commas,
I create my voice.
Into the abyss I leap and land where I want,
Without using a grammar check.
I like to dominate the rules,
To infringe them between ellipses.
What would be rules,
If they weren't meant to be broken?
I build my world,
Centered in a spiral of wisdom.
Squeezing the experience out of life,
With the flavor of honey.
I beat my wings,
I climb the hillside,
Between mountains and valleys,
I fly above life's creations.
But life,
My life,
I am the one who chooses
The best way to live!

for Rita

Wings

I created a dream,
One that flew far.
I opened a door and gave it wings.
I followed it like a mother follows a son,
Without knowing his destination.
I watched it grow and mature,
And finally depart.
I waited,
And one day he returned,
To grow old by my side.

for Tomás

Ladybug

Fly, fly, Ladybug.
Without ever stopping.
You are a wise beauty, Ladybug.
Who came to teach us!

Fly, fly, Ladybug.
Always with assurance Ladybug.
Flying in a straight line,
Never straying from your path.

Fly, fly, Ladybug.
On your unwavering flight Ladybug.
It's you who knows,
Where to land!

Fly, fly, Ladybug.
Come and get my love,
Fly, fly, Ladybug.
And take me with you to Lisbon!

for Joana

Wisdom

Wisdom flies,
It has wings to depart,
Has wings to come back.
Wisdom takes us to the other side.

The wind blows:
Wisdom has wings,
It knows how to leave at the right moment,
Taking along only a song.

for Sofia

Flight 27

Enigmas

That morning,
The sea opened up.
The storm spread across the sky,
Waves with the smell of power,
A sea that turned into sky,
A sky that turned into earth.
In the midst of the storm
I discovered my voice.
It arrived serene,
Calm,
Sweet,
With the taste of honey.
With the wings of birds,
It flew through open spaces,
And showed me without wavering
New horizons.
I felt the fear of flying.
I called out to my ancestor for
Stories that could bring me certainty,
Certainties that no one could give,
Until the risk of flight was ventured.
The lightness of being, lifted me.
I closed my eyes and confronted this new space,
New stories to tell,
Enigmas to decipher.

My Song

With these short words,
I sing my pain,
Because I don't know how to cry.
I sing my joy,
With all the letters and syllables.

In the ballad of the night,
Or when I awaken to the day,
I adjust my compass.
I know what I feel,
Or imagine what I don't.

With these short words,
I translate the flight of the bird,
That soars above emotions,
Without knowing where to land.

Identity

I take three hearts with me,
Each one with its own color.
Don't ask me to choose,
Each one has its own place.

At the end of my life I will look back.
In each path a love,
On each trail a nationality,
But in all, I learned how to walk.

I take with me only one flag,
True to my own self,
Planted high on a mountain.
I will call it my life
And say thank you to God!

Star

I am here,
Transported,
Through dimensions,
Of the universe.

I sense a scent,
I see the moon,
And watch the sunrise.

I follow the star of my heart.

Flight 31

The Secret

The secret exists in silence,
Closed in the quietest parts of the soul,
A moment of inner journey,
Without color, without sound, without smell.
The secret reveals itself,
Evoking feelings,
Alive sensations,
Transformed into a new road
to follow. . .
in secret!

for Graciela

Trail

You are right,
I don't have a poem to give,
Only small words to dedicate to you.
I want to give you the sun, the moon and the stars,
But our path is a trail already paved,
That only can be traveled with you.
Stone layered on stone,
Day after day,
Night after night,
A life with Love,
In which I met you.

You are right,
I don't have a poem to give you,
Only a life to share.

for Eduardo

Leonor Alvim Brazão

Leonor was born in Lisbon, Portugal, but spent her youth
in Brazil where she studied visual arts, music, and dance.
She obtained a degree in Visual Communication from
Mackenzie University and a postgraduate degree
in Arts Education from the Centro Universitário Claretiano.
Upon her return to Lisbon, Leonor began a career in advertising
where she worked for several creative agencies.
Currently, she lives in the United States where
she exhibits her artwork regularly.
She is a visual artist, graphic designer, poet, educator
and works for an art education company.